Smoke in the Afterlife

Smoke in the Afterlife

Emilio Iasiello

SMOKE IN THE AFTERLIFE

Copyright © 2019 Emilio Iasiello

First Edition, 2019. All rights reserved.

A Thurston Howl Publications Book

Published by Thurston Howl Publications
thurstonhowlpublications.com
Lansing, MI

jonathan.thurstonhowlpub@gmail.com

Printed in the United States of America
10 9 8 7 6 5 4 3 2 1

For Carmen, Betta, and Mimmuccio who give me the time to write.

"*In every dispute between parent and child, both cannot be right, but they may be, and usually are, both wrong. It is this situation which gives family life its peculiar hysterical charm.*"
—Isaac Rosenfeld

I

That Sunday

I remember you best in the living room
that Sunday, your hand loose
around the bottle's neck,
disturbed gin breath
trailing from your open mouth.
I remember tip-toeing toward you,
careful not to creak the wood floor
beneath me,
watching you recede
into the tethered net of sleep.
It was difficult to imagine you angry,
so relaxed and boneless in that chair,
hard to believe it was you who raised the belt
with its ugly buckle against your son,
windmilling lash after lash
for the broken ashtray or the spilled milk,
the girlie magazine tucked under the mattress.
Hard to believe it was you
who volunteered at the hospital,
made sure each sick child had something
to open on Christmas, and not the same woman
who forgot that her youngest son's birthday
was the twenty-eighth and not the twenty-ninth.
That Sunday, I remember standing over you, Mother,
a bruised bundle of eight-year-old hate,

and in that moment
every scar you put on me seemed to scream
in chorus
this is how I love you, let me
count the ways.

Angels on the Head of a Pin

I used to dream of angels—their blurred forms
in the moments after sleep, wings rising high above
rounded shoulders like clouds or snow-tipped peaks.
I'd lie in bed, and they would come, one
by one, a sky of longing haloed in each tender eye.
One day, I set out to find miracles, entered
morning, and returned when the sky grew red,
my shirt flecked with burrs and mud, thorn
scratches on my legs. I told my mother I was searching
for angels, and she laughed, bunching my clothes as she
ran a bath. Once, I saw shadows in my room, dark in their bulk,
and all around me the soundlessness of feathers filling
the wedges and corners with their trembling silk. I watched
them unfold in the loose spaces, bolts of white cloth
left to unravel like hair released from a barrette. And when
I woke from a nightmare, shadow contrasted against
the inattentive darkness, not the closet door left ajar,
but children with wings. I called for my mother and told her
what I'd seen, and she came in, incensed, pin in hand, pointing
to its head: here are your angels. I didn't understand,
although they drifted from me a little further each night after,
a memory that is neither anger nor joy, but somehow less real.
All I could hear was her voice, still as a ray of light,
your angels dance on the head of a pin, her words
an unbroken spell circling the air. All around me, I felt their
deaths break down into questions whose answers hinted at nothing
and drew apart from me like the ground raked clean of the ice
that encases it; the surface left cold, scored, abandoned.

Passing Roadkill in August

(A family trip)
My face is twisted
impossibly away
from my body,
the cry still trapped
in my throat.
If it came now,
would you hear it,
would you understand
that I once loved motion,
the moon, the thin
night air?
Could you have watched
the road better,
one eye fixed
on my midnight passage,
the other on that tar river
that twists into nothingness
caked in nothingness;
cracked the window for breath,
considered my destination:
the cubs, the den,
my home?
Did you cringe
at the hollow sound—
my body a momentary bump
in the night—
recognize those long,

sad moments
between fear and guilt?
Stranger
speeding away
from the source of her crime—
your voice is disguised.
Your tears
aren't even real.

My Brother Speaks

My brother's face
the year before prep school: sun beaming
off pale skin, early spring.
The night before, we had lain in silence,
listening for our mother's Chevy to scatter the darkness.
I'm leaving,
you said, turning your back to me, feigning sleep
as we did when she came into our room late,
her breath steeped in gin. The next day,
you took me outside, afraid
our spoons and cereal bowls
would shatter her sleep, pitch her into jabs
and punches, the twisting of the deranged.
I watched you fight for the words, not able to tell
your younger brother the reasons why, eyes searching
the lawn as if something in the earth
could resolve my grief. I can't forget that morning,
the air sweetened with freshly cut grass,
the dogwoods trapped in mid-bloom; each bulb
a puff of blown glass. And when you looked up,
the sun blinded you for an instant,
closing your eyes as if that could justify
your move away, pawning that damned torch off
on another, leaving me to fill those terrible, empty shoes.

The Beating

I never forgave you for that Monday
two days before my brother left for prep school,
walking into the house
to find you at the kitchen table, the gin bottle
resting on its side as if waiting
for a ship to be built inside its belly.
You exploded to your feet, the back of your hand
catching my face, your diamond's edge
cutting into my skin, your fingers streaked in blood.
On my knees, I felt the hate of your nails
dig into my back, my t-shirt transformed
into rags with two vicious tugs. You unleashed
the leather belt with its unforgiving buckle
filling the kitchen with each crack and thud,
the walls absorbing my cries like a priest
absorbing confession. And when your eyebrows
released themselves from that dark position
in your face, you left the room with me huddled
on the floor like a junkie in need of a fix,
walking past me as if I were no relation,
as if the blood from my veins
was different from yours.

My Brother Leaves

You packed up for boarding school
before she got worse, took your cleats,
your books, the last good picture
of Father. Your room became
less you and more her, starkness
reclaiming space the way nature
reclaimed the land, moving in that slow,
deliberate push. She had grown silent
after his death, sipping gin while we ate supper,
becoming dark and strange, a volcano. You must
have seen it then, the lava in her eyes,
the mood swings, the alcohol. You must
have sensed something I couldn't, and deciding
it would be better so, you left, slipping away
unscathed like water through the fingers.
On the bus, you just stared ahead
like someone leaving the old country—
without looking back, burning
in anticipation for the new world ahead.

For My Brother Who Needs Strength

Consider Theseus
as he first stepped
into the labyrinth,
his seventeen boy years
frozen onto his face
like a scar. Then consider
his fear as the door closed,
burying him in shadow
while his old man
picked his teeth
with splintered bone.
And remember how Theseus,
with two balled fists,
stalked through that maze,
breathing in the stale air,
his teeth gripped with hate
until he beat the bull,
until he beat the bull
who was his shadow,
tunneling punch after punch
into that black beast.
And with that,
you must realize
how, for one small moment,
Theseus held everything
in his hands,
bringing down a certain finality
with every arc of his fist,

ridding himself
of that hell forever.
Theseus walked away
from that maze
because he was free.
He walked away
because he had earned
the right
to step into sun.

Scorpio Child

Scorpio, maligned sign,
jealous spider, you lead me
to the darker side,
October's leaves crunching
beneath your legs and mine.
Tonight, the sky burns
with stars,
and our claws nip
their tiny buds, tails
curling to question marks
above our heads, the sweet
poison dripping
from the jagged barbs. They curve
toward the passion of Mars,
aggressive to plunge
our sting
deep within that hot planet,
and feel within its tremble
the promise of rebirth,
while we relax
in the fading aftermath,
content in our self-discovery,
transformed,
ready to live again.

EMILIO IASIELLO

Mischief Night

Before midnight, before the vagrant pander
of children for candy, before any solicitation whatsoever,
we'd play tricks so the neighbors
would remember treats. My friend and I
and a dozen eggs slipped from house
to house, soaping up windows, draping toilet paper
off trees, two-ply white tinsel. We smeared
shaving cream on handles, rang doorbells,
chalked sidewalks. We moved without conscience,
striking like matches in flames of indifference.
We shook everything apart. We burned
in the night, reproduced gestures
that thumbed their noses at the world as if to say,
here, take that.

October

The wind is cut with witches' laughter,
cold as a newt-
skin or spider web,
or whatever gets cast into a cauldron
this time of year, *bubble, bubble,*
toil and trouble. Outside,
goblins pander house
to house. The vampire
and his younger ghouls
from next door who sent a baseball
through the window last spring
lug their sacks up the walk.
They ring our house in search
of Snickers, trick or treat,
mischief's threat gleaming
beneath pancake and rouge,
youthful eyes.
What's sweet to the teeth
is a night heaped
with candy, mouths pressed
with the urge for chocolate,
caramel, *give me something good*
to eat they holler
when I open the door.
And I do.

Witch

This evening, I've made peace
with my shadows and this house
that consumes them; the twisted
coil of steps that leads
to a bed that knows one imprint,
one weight, the pillow, one head.
I have watched children
through my window, flapping house
to house, bats churning in endless night.
They skitter around drunk on sugar,
webbed in sheets, masks,
ketchup splattered on one shirt, mock blood.
Each year, it's the same:
werewolf, vampire, skeleton
stirred in a pack like ingredients
for a spell. They pass on my
candle-less pumpkin, as if to stare
too long at an empty place
is to become what you fear.
They don't realize
that love is a season made desolate
with the dismissal of what lives.
Love is the grief that knocks
and the hollow
that knocks back.

The Joker

Fall. October 31. Halloween. A night
for mischief and lawlessness, for candy,
for scaring children younger than yourself,
and not to be afraid when it's your dead father's face
you see in every mask. Three days past my birthday,
it's the snap and growl of the season, my mother
returning to the bottle like a shark to waters
where feeding is good. She smears cream
on my face, her breath crisp with Tanquery
and ice, bloodshot eyes branching off into red tributaries.
Her breath is all cigarette. It's not
the vampire's creased grin she paints,
nor the werewolf's darkened veins flexed
in the cry for blood, for blood,
but a lopsided face, a clown, the joker,
the person who's supposed to laugh,
the laugh you can't forget.

First Thanksgiving after Father's Death

Everything is as it should be: forks, knives,
linen napkins folded neatly over each plate,
candles rising like white phalluses toward God,
candied yams which are my favorite, biscuits hot enough
to melt butter before Grace can be said (my brother's favorite),
mashed potatoes, corn. My brother back from prep school sits
at Daddy's place at the table. He looks small in the powerful chair,
the way children look small in their parent's clothing.
Mother finally comes in with turnips and squash,
just in case, she says, as if the meal on the table
was barely fit for ten and not a family of three.
That afternoon, we sat in silence, feeding off
each other's lives, lifting forkful after forkful
of memory into our hungry mouths, devouring the need
settled so firmly within us, a need
that, after seven months of wanting, none of us
could satisfy.

Fifteenth Birthday

It was a day like any other; the house
filled with stillness and fear, my mother
asleep on the couch, unconscious from a fifth
of gin. Shadows grew large and strange
in the corners, the only sound stumbling
from my mother's drunken lips.
I stopped resisting long ago and came
to accept her anger as easily as the belt
she liked to use; accepted her gin
and her spite, her forgetfulness
and indifference. I turned fifteen
with the wisdom of one who has been beaten
so many times, his scars served
as both penance and confession.
I breathed and suffocated under her presence.
I measured her love in stitches and welts.
I endured.
Fifteen years old, I grabbed
the bottle from her open hand.
I took my first drink.

Retelling the Story

Because my mother taught little
and what she taught I did not believe,
I took matters into my own hands;
saved the money from Christmas,
walked down the road forbidden me to travel,
past the strippers and the bruised faces
of the drunks, past boarded-up dives
where my grandfather blew sax,
straight to the lady on the corner—
fishnet, leather, makeup
thick as frosting.
Her room was small and angular;
mattress torn, stuffing sticking out—
a swollen tongue. Heat clanked
through the pipes, the working-class anthem.
She peeled the dress from her body
the way my grandfather peeled an apple,
careful to keep the skin in one piece,
her flesh white as an apple's meat.
She snaked toward me,
smile stretched across her mouth,
hands slipping under my shirt,
her experienced touch
undoing my confusions like buttons;
moving past the flared cheeks, the shyness,
breath strained and tight;

past the innocence, to the place
where, for one rigid instant,
everything made sense.
Laying there, the roaches circling
like a herald of angels,
I remember thinking how my mother was right;
I had found neither the Kingdom
nor the Kingdom Come.

Better

Now that I think of it, it was better
that there was never another, no third son
to burden a leather belt across the back,
to feel the skin rise like biscuits
in the oven, the blood hot and pumping.
It was better that you never conceived again,
Daddy dying too shortly after marriage, cancer
devouring him until his flesh sagged sickly
from the bone. Eight years old, I remember him
in the hospital bed, watching
the thin smile slip from his mouth,
his teeth yellow to the root. He had wanted
a younger brother for me, but when he died
I knew it was for a purpose. It was better
that only I saw you all those years
jailed in that liquid dungeon,
your body taut with gin,
eyes worn and scalloped. Better that I alone
watched you stumble and scream, throw
bottle after bottle against the wall,
glass exploding in a fountain of stars.
It was better that there was only me
fulfilling a promise of a child
to his dying father, a promise to take care of
and protect, but most of all, a promise
to survive, to survive.

Becoming My Mother

It was bound to happen. After all those years
watching her tilt gin to her swollen mouth
and listening to the cool pull and swallow;
I have become my mother. I have become
that woman, ranting with the wine-stain
on her cheek no larger than a dime,
full breasted as a dove, spirited, sad.
I have found myself in her skin,
seethed with her rage, bloomed with the proud
flower of her sex, succumbed to its passion.
I have turned my coal-hard eyes
against the world and met its stare
measure for measure, listened to its songs
and grievances, ignored its tender cries.
I have even fed from her bottle, beaten
a path inside her toward the landless dark,
to find the place where she hides,
to understand why she doesn't leave.

Our Names in Blood

You took the blade and waved it
over the flame, the metal
heating up, blackening, smoke
twisting in angry, grey coils.
You grabbed my wrist, pressing
the point down, *this is forever*, you said,
carving slowly. I watched
the blood surface
in an awkward smile, the way
I'm sure my mouth looked four years later
when the tattoo needle
dug into my ankle, the bird
spreading its dark wings feather by feather,
another pledge to another friend.
And when I see the puckered skin,
the paint, I think of us that night
passing vodka back and forth,
sucking on filter-less cigarettes
until our lungs ached from their martyred rapture,
your pocket knife tipped red,
the wing of a blackbird. We pressed
our wrists together, the virgules
sealing themselves like the hushed
mouths of sinners waiting
for something voiceless,
something intact.

Trimming Dinner Lettuce

Shaving these green skulls,
I investigate the white matter of each
tiny cerebellum; my fingers crawl,
peeling away layers of each emerald cartilage.
These heads bear the scars and dirt
of underground labor. Conceived from the same dust
and water that sprouted flesh and marrow.
The same dust that hugged these green embryos.
The same dust that my father's bones have become.

Weeding

On Saturday, the day of chores,
long afternoons, and summertime heat,
my brother and I weed
the flower beds.
He squats down like a catcher,
his fingers separating
bud from weed,
and because I am younger,
and because I still mind his words,
I rake the yellow eyes
of the daisies into a pile.
Tomorrow, he leaves this job
for good. He knows
he will never have to carve a home
for mums and lilies
out of crab grass and rock.
He turns the soil softly
over in his hands,
smiles because it reminds him
of Father.
When he's done, what's left
are the violets we planted this May—
the dirt under our nails
and the fading ache
of bee stings.
I lift the bag of weeds
over my shoulder,

my brother next to me in silence.
Next year, this will be
my obligation. But for now,
we leave the beds together,
respecting the peace
my brother alone has given them.

Childhood Rushes Toward Death

I picture you, mother, as a girl
growing up on Tom Thumb Street,
smoking discarded butts
behind the garage,
sneaking that first drink—
and Grandpa, who chose the saxophone
over the slow hours, stitching leather soles
into shoes, collecting pocket change.
Standing there on stage,
cheeks puffed to the point of bursting,
he blew hot riffs to the waitresses who wrote
their bust sizes on matchbooks
and slipped them down his front pocket,
their perfume and cigarette stench,
his elixir.
And then there's Grandma who endured
with a quiet resilience,
fixed to the routine of a four-room house,
her love measured by the hands
that cooked and cleaned for her family.
She'd spend the night sewing by the window,
listening for footsteps that never sounded,
thinking alone, hoping.
I consider how hard it was on you,
putting the favored sister through college,
mending shoes until two in the morning
at your father's shop,
saving nothing for yourself. How, one night,

you rammed an awl almost clean through
your palm, trying to see if this was your life
and not some horrible dream imagined.
Most of all, I think of your face that day
as the clear fluid touched
the back of your throat, the fire
exploding inside your belly,
the coughing, the spitting,
the lightheadedness that flooded
your mind. I look into
that girl's face, mother,
and realize that it was death
she was looking for
when she took that first drink.

Anniversary of my Father's Death

It's late. I sit next to you in the tortured house
of my childhood, sipping the gin
you taught me to drink. You refill your glass
for the fifth time, a ritual you have
perfected these past fifteen years,
your hand pouring and emptying, pouring
and emptying, a gesture worth repeating.
We don't speak.
I sat in a similar silence in the hospital
when my father was dying,
his body wrung out and twisted
like hand-washed laundry. His body
had given up, reducing itself
like a Chinese doll that sheds its shell
in favor of the diminutive replica.
I watched his eyes slip from blue
to black, listened as his breath
surrendered to the cancer that had laced
his lungs with phlegm.
I remember holding his hand,
that thin skeleton, feeling his grip lessen
as his heart eventually straightened out
and relaxed.
Your hand is equally thin,
the fingers fine like breadsticks.
You are no longer that woman thrown easily
into fits, fed on anger, explosive.
For the first time in my life,

I see you as one who has waited
for a moment that has never come;
one filled with imperfection and regret,
you, this woman,
my mother.

You, Sick

in bed, the covers
gathered around your waist
in large, paisley folds.
Your forehead rages with fever
against my palm, your breath
breaking with congestion,
the struggle of the lungs.
Six o'clock, and the cold
surfaces again, snow outside
hardening on the ground
like frosting exposed
to the air too long. I spoon
soup into your mouth, blowing on
the broth before bringing it
to your dry lips. You cry
to be well again. I know
what it's like to wait alone,
watching shadows grow
and shrink against the wall,
the room steadily goldening.
I know what it's like
to shiver beneath
down covers, orange juice
thick on my tongue like blood,
the room reduced to stale air
and sweat where your scabrous voice
unravels in the dark.

Crow, Alone

(My mother's self-portrait)

No one sees her on the rubble
of the house, collapsed
into itself, reduced
to a common denominator
of brick
and wood; no one that stops to say,—
look, a crow,
then watches as she cranes her neck
in understanding of the sight
before her, an endless array
of charred stone and ash,
the erasures of what
an instant of light can bring.
And as she skitters across
the debris,
chains of people
pass her by, their flesh scorched
and patched as torn orange rinds,
and she just teeters there,
flapping her singed wings,
unable to catch the currents
to lift her into the splintered
ruin of daylight.

31

Mother at Fifty

I know what you think even though
your brown eyes screen your anguish,
the uncertainty of thought
inscribed in your smile as you sit
for the flashes, firing one after
another like heat lightening.
The human condition is to worry
over the choices we've made,
to perpetually exist outside ourselves,
and think what would be
if we weren't here at this instant,
wondering if our happiness
and the path not taken are, in fact,
inextricable. And it's at this confusion
that we must recognize that hope rests
in what we have and not what we have
given up, that we are reborn
in moments of weakness when we apply
ourselves to the possibilities of existence,
and draw from our own necessity
and triumph to become something greater,
so we might meet the future as it comes
into view, the light of our fate
woven around us—we wouldn't falter,
we would know everything.

Repentance

You lay in your death
beyond the rambling of prayer
where your religion bathes you
in false prophecy.
Why look to Christ?
Pinned to the prison
of that damned cross,
knee-deep in aching abandonment.
And yet this crucifix
in my hands
is strangely familiar,
like a childhood toy
lost and rediscovered,
and I finger each individual bead,
knowing the depth
of the myth I touch
touches the place
in your body that leans
toward spiritual fulfillment.
And I have tried
to lean with you, all those days
when you read to me
Revelations and Genesis,
but I turned from those words
because there was no lesson,
because they were nothing more
than stories.
And I hold this crucifix

you gave to me
when you told me to believe,
and I am sorry,
but I can't believe
anymore that I can raise you
out of that bed like Lazarus.
Know that, in the end,
I searched my own head
and found neither prophets
nor fire to follow;
only the delusions of the weary,
people like you
believing that single
great, complicated lie.

II

The Moment

My father as I best remember him—
Sunday afternoons by our house, late August,
the afternoon light surrendering to dusk.
This was time away from his patients,
away from that white building he vanished into
when I wouldn't see him for days,
time for me, the second son,
his spitting image.
We moved past familiar landscape—
St. Margaret's Shrine and the market that stayed open
late just for him, past neighborhood women pushing
strollers in which babies he had delivered slept;
who was late, who had the Cesarean,
each child its own complicated story.
And when my mother asks me now,
I tell her how, on one particular evening,
we came upon a small boy crying,
a petal of skin missing above one knee,
his bicycle turned over and twisted,
a machine too difficult to master. And I tell her
how he bent down and soothed the boy
with his voice, dabbing the wound clean
with a handkerchief, always smiling, tender, careful.
I stood and watched him send that boy
back off on his bike, a messenger carrying

the Good News, and I remember my father
turning toward me, our eyes meeting
as if to impart to me a secret—
the shining look of one
who has experienced the miracle.

The Gift

When I was six, my father
brought me a stethoscope for my birthday,
not a child's toy, but a real physician's tool—
the metal polished brightly like a new Lincoln penny.
It had always been on his mind,
a second doctor in the family,
so he concentrated on his youngest,
the ideal apprentice—even the name was identical,
a perfect fit. I spent the entire day
with it around my neck, listening to the refrain
of my heart. The son, the son
it beat out, drumming the same tune
my father had heard in Italy
when his father delivered a baby boy.
He held the infant close to him so he could hear
the steady thump of blood and muscle,
the pushing fluid, the music of the body.
This is what he wanted to say,
but how do you explain that to one so young?
What I did not understand, I listened to,
watching my father's face as he hunched forward,
eyes burning with the excitement
of one whose gift was made from his own two hands;
formed through hours of love and patience;
raised in awe; staring in fever and wonder
at its creation.

Fisherman's Son

(A painting in my father's office)
All that remains
is to carry the last of the fish
from the boat. He stands
up to his ankles in folding water,
heaving the hollowed carcass—
a lifetime's work—
onto the sun-blanched sand.
His white beard bronzes
in the dying light, and he smiles,
knowing the harvest
he has caught that day will turn
a good price at market.
In the distance, he sees
his youngest son running
down the beach,
the thin, brown arms stretched wide
as if to swallow the entire sea
with his love. *Papa, papa,*
vieni qui, come here, he hears—
his voice a gull's shrill cry
above water. Behind him,
footsteps dissipate in a sweep
of foam and thunder, and he leaps
into the old man's hands,
his body elegant and smooth
as the ray and this old man clutches
onto this child, this small fragment

that is his life, as if he was Christ
blessing the last fish
on the mountain top,
trying to transform a mouth-full
into food for a lifetime,
raising his person to the sea
for approval:
this is my son,
he comes to you from me.

The Apology

My father never apologized for his patients
or the house calls he made late at night;
when a patient hurts, he would say,
there is only need. There were days
when he lived in name only,
trapped at the hospital, that diseased cage,
visiting the beneficiaries of his love.
I hadn't seen him in over a week
when he walked through the door once,
ruffled and worn as a bird caught
in a storm. I remember
how the flesh hung from his cheeks
as if sleep had been wrenched
from his face, his jaw slack and lifeless.
He looked at me, then collapsed into a chair,
its wide back rising from his shoulders like wings,
a fallen angel, and slept, still as a rock
imbedded in moss. When he finally awoke
hours later, it was his agonized touch upon my back—
one whose realization is loss. I gazed back
at my father beginning the early stages of his death,
his eyes sleep-crusted, kneeling down
to offer up his soul in apology,
waiting for it to be taken the way they said
it would be taken—without condition
or surrender—the wronged would kiss his cheek,
all would be forgiven.

My Father Asleep

When it would be a day like any other,
a sick child, a pregnancy,
another family with another need,
my father would uproot himself
from the table, the black bag
that was his love in hand, and disappear
down the front porch steps.
Sometimes, I would awaken in the morning
to a saw buzzing and find my father asleep
in his big chair, mouth ajar, snoring,
his clothes wrinkled like tired skin,
fold upon fold of exhaustion.
I liked him best this way,
no longer intimidating in the gray flannel
he wore like an armor suit,
his face, relaxed and lineless,
sucking in great gulps of air.
I would get close to him
and smell his day-old aftershave,
rub my cheek against the roughness
of the man who was my namesake,
to see him stir as if touched by a dream
too real, then slip beneath the unconscious again.
Sometimes, I would watch him sleep all afternoon,
coal pressed in leather,
and witness the man who cured everyone
helpless under deep slumber,
the raw humanity of his heart beating

I am, I am, I am.

The Sentinel

As a boy, I remember those nights
when the telephone sliced its awful ring
through our sleep: hearing you
get up to answer it, the floor groaning
beneath your feet. There was no hesitation—
a patient was sick—and so you stole away
from your wife's side, abandoning her in bed
like a prostitute paid for the done deed.
Perhaps it was too easy for you—too routine—
like passing a flower without smelling it,
sure to find it on the way back
fixed in its position, unchanged.
My mother would rise, padding softly down
to the living room sofa to stand watch,
waiting,
listening for your engine's grind
down the hill. Only then
would she climb back into bed, masking herself
in sleep before you slipped between the sheets
two hours before dawn.
I wonder if you ever knew
how she kept vigil by a window
three quarters full of night,
staying by her post for your return, dutiful,
this sentinel of love.

Market

Here at the diner,
I think of Tegucigalpa
as a place where things
suddenly begin. Where vendors jockey
through working-class streets
and flesh presses against flesh;
where the hustle to sell rises
in a stench of sweat and fruit,
each twisted face sunburned
and fractured from dryness.
Where need is translated into
the rattle of bananas and linens,
and voices hoarse with capitalism,
todo barato, todo bueno--
everything cheap, everything good quality.
I imagine you walking
to market with other students,
pockets heavy
with *lempira* and *centavos,*
anxious to absorb, to contemplate...
to watch streets fill with people
caught between living
and that something other.
Somewhere on a corner,
a woman six-months pregnant
pleads for food.
Once in Rome,
I watched an old woman wrapped

in a *serape* rock a sick child
in her arms, her hand out,
palm uplifted.
She spent the entire day
pinching coins and crumpled paper.
At night, she left
in a dark Mercedes
and disappeared down the road.
It's crazy like this.
How to know what to give?
Whose voice do you listen to...whose cry?
You surrender a dollar or two.
The market pulses
in a maddening frenzy.
You sense the intoxication,
the urgency, the cut-throat
savvy.
Between two extremes,
there is something trapped in the middle.
Guess it.

September Evening

It's night. The stars are bedded above us,
tucked into that thick, black blanket,
their tiny, white eyes poking through.
Sitting on the grass, our naked thighs touch
in a reverent kiss. It's too easy to say nothing,
to lie back and watch the silence grow
like Faust, conjuring those giddy shadows
to do our bidding. Tonight, the darkness holds
a fleeting sound, that low susurrus rising
through the leaves, bustling their rough skins,
that certain harmony, distinct in its fullness,
spiraling above us in windswept arcs, quiet
as a whisper, propelled into that soft, accepting light.

The Aftermath

We watched
with the curiosity
of children
the falling snow
and how each flake
descended
with the eloquence
of an angel's sigh.
Looking out
from beneath
our warmth,
the ground
whitened over
like powdered sugar
while two crows
danced
against an empty
sky, pirouetting
like drunken marionettes.
Holding you,
I felt the lapsed
movements
of time, the comfort
of your mouth
pressed
against mine
while
two dark birds

circled around
and around,
waiting for that magic
to happen.

So You Can See Me,

I lie beneath the digital, ribbed glow
of the clock. Your silhouette undresses
shirt-pants-socks, the light from the hall
burning your image like a radiation flash.
You peer through the blinds to see
the first fragments blur past the window
while somewhere your friend and her family
ski down a mountain. In another room,
their dog breathes heavily in sleep.
Somewhere outside, a sick howl
knifes through the trees. If I could
capture a moment, I would paint you
like this—calm and unafraid, looking out
at the gathering whiteness with one palm
pressed against the glass of a window
resistant to the cold of the wind.

The Product

I was made from your mold,
pressed into your image, a clay figure
put together piece by piece. Humming softly,
you set out to create yourself,
so you laid everything out carefully—
tools, water, silt,
the gray mass of your making.
You spent the entire day on this,
the second son, kneading each part
knowing that the result depends so much
on its beginning. Softening the material,
you pinched and edged, scored the hair
until just right, widened the face,
dimpled the chin. You shaped each feature,
sweat bathing you in a fluorescent sheen,
your eye marvelous with creation, a phony god.
Finished, you carved your name into me,
signing the way a sculptor does
when he's ready to show his product to the world.

The Lie

Those final stages,
my father lay in the hospital,
the tubes removed from his nose
and mouth,
his breath falling in harshened gasps.
He waved me over,
his sluggish arm bruised
from IV marks, thinned by cancer,
and I stood beside him,
oblivious to the pain I mistook
in his eye for a smile. I remember
searching for an answer
to a question that stagnated
on my lips, the strangeness
clenched tightly in my stomach,
a fist of uncertainty.
It couldn't be asked, even now,
my father and I alone in the room,
years and silence between us.
Each time I tried to speak, I stopped,
relying on my mother's faith,
words that made for simple answers,
simple promises, something a child
could hold onto for strength.
When I left that man,
I kissed his cheek one last time,
and in that consciousness,
he raised a thumb skyward in his only lie to me:
Everything is fine. I will always be there.

Smile, Anger, Kisses

When I remember my father, it's not
his face I see—that tortured look—saint-like—
stained in the windows at church, eyes cast downward
in agony, a halo pulsing above his head—
not the tired thread of his song
hummed softly those Sunday mornings in his favorite chair,
paper steepled neatly over his chest.
And when I dream him now at night,
It's not really my father, but what I can't quite touch,
his undefined presence, a leap of faith.
To remember my father, I must go back
to a child's understanding of a parent
he fears and loves and imitate each movement
through the house—shaving with him in the bathroom,
mimicking his long razor strokes with my popsicle stick,
cringing beneath the after-shave splashed
onto my cheeks, *per le raggazze*, he'd say,
for the girls. And because he died when I was young,
it is difficult to recount each detail of his life:
the sound his shoes made on the sidewalk
when he returned home from work, or the glasses
continually misplaced on his head,
the breath he made when he passed away.
And so, when asked if I remember *il dottore*,
I remember his smile, his anger, and his kisses,
my father in all three forms—
what greeted me every morning,
the crease in his brow at my negligence,

and what I took to sleep with me each night;
the way he would hoist me onto his shoulders
to view the world from his level,
the way it was endless.

Coffee

Before you left, I said
you were too beautiful for me.
That much is still true.
The wonder I feel when you sit across
from me sipping coffee
is the same fear that claws up my spine
when I think of you in Guatemala now—
sharing the afternoon light with some *guapo*
street side, the espresso cup
pressed firmly between your capable fingers—
or maybe
drinking plain ol' American
with another student
missing his girlfriend as much
as you miss me,
a candle flame between you,
its small confession in light—
discovering in a mistake of passion
that loneliness
is what's uncovered with your hands,
its heightened breath on your neck,
a touch or two.
I know it's foolish,
but my life is spent thinking
one day, praying the next.
I stare at the stained ring
in my cup, the bitter grounds
stuck mercilessly to the bottom,

and I suddenly think, *hot,*
black, as if there's no better way
to torture myself.
When I drink coffee,
I'm really
trading one life for another.

Poem for an Unknown Father

Each night for a week in Rome,
your brothers writhed with the pain
of memory, silence swallowing up their voices
as the sky swallows up the screams of the dead.
I sat untangling their words from me,
the room filling with endless shadow
like a flower unfolding itself petal by petal.
I expected you to resurrect yourself
from their mouths in a tongue of flame,
circle my head in a fire's wreath
like some holy ghost mad with prophecy.
For one week, they conjured up
images from ashes and old photographs.
I listened to your name chant
through the air, a lost prayer,
waited for it to touch me as a rosary,
with a light pat above the heart.
Now, when I think of the dead and religion
I remember that night
I stayed up until six am,
dawn's skin stretching around me,
waiting for that sign to believe,
that one shred of proof.

Watching Home Movies

My father rolls his trousers
to the knees, the August humidity
thick on his legs with grass balm and sweat.
He rocks my crib back and forth
as he mouths the words to *il topolino*,
a child's song about the presence of fear.
Behind him, a boy steals the scene
when a car skids into frame, gray-black
like the unseen hand that snatches
the mouse in the final stanza, its last breath
trapped between those improvident fingers.
What comes next is natural.
My father sprints to the boy,
kneels, listens to his chest,
fingers the pulse. He breathes
oxygen into the windpipe,
filling the tiny lungs—
a pair of tattered water wings
expanding
and retreating. He lifts the body
into the ambulance, closes the door.
Concerned, he watches it reduce
to a gray point on the horizon.
This is my father as I've known him
all my life, preoccupied amid the confusion,
lost among well-wishers who have witnessed
another generosity,

EMILIO IASIELLO

while his infant lies abandoned
in the front yard, the emptiness slipping
over him; his futile fingers
clawing the darkening sky.

Falmouth Heights

What mattered for the moment
was something
that even we didn't understand,
the movement along the shores
of our deepest fears, that brought us here,
in the waning light, two forms strapped
in the desire to possess something more,
something outside the ordinary.
And perhaps it was the wish
to feel beyond the darkness
that we stood shoulders touching,
searching the night sky for images
of ourselves, the black folding
of a starless region
in the distance, the sweep
of a magnificent and lightless sea.
And we stood before it
as if, by recognizing its existence,
it became ours, and its wind
was our wind, and its sound
became the oldest sound we knew,
until it came over us
in a ruminant hum, and we basked
in its glow, letting its dark breath
run over our upturned faces, feeling
that we possessed the power
to imagine beyond our bodies—
that was the secret.

Night Song

At this hour, I listen
to the sound her fingers make
when they touch ivory.
Its Beethoven tonight, *Fur Elise,*
music that outlasts my breath,
and I imagine the way she kisses
must be the way Beethoven imagined
when he exiled himself to write
the tender sway of this piece,
the snowy plume of his quill
catching the night's tremble.
And as she plays, it's not so much
the spirit of the notes
as the curve of her neck
where the deepened light rests,
where the hour transcribes
the pregnancy of sound
and evening threads the reticence
of the widening dark—auspices,
crickets, the air made soft with shadow.
If there is beauty, it exists
beyond imagination
or moments where nothing is lacking:
the unbroken spell of her fingers
moving in a love
I wish I possessed, its song hovering,
flourishing like a dream of words
that goes on proposing.

Letter from My Dead Father

All you need tell me of yourself is that you still are—
the rest remains with me in sleep where memory
is whatever one chooses: a photograph, a song,
a lingering touch from a loved one. You are thirty now,
older than the child who first felt my life slip
between his fingers so many years ago,
and, when I look at that boy,
I remember the words that fell silent on my lips
like an echo dissipating in the night air.
Since you wonder, most days I recall
by an ill child's embrace, or kisses planted on my knuckles
from old women, their saliva like medicine
on my skin. My life I define by this—
what more can you give?
A carpenter builds, a priest prays, but only a doctor loves.
Each day, someone comes into your hands
as if your touch is strength, and each day,
your palms press against them to heal, to heal.
Of this, I am certain—there is magic in the moment
light enters the body, travelling through each limb,
and magic in the moment of recovery
when the eyes emerge from sleepy depths.
I have watched them climb the slow journey
upward, trapped in their bodies' oceans,
balanced between free-fall and prayer.
I have seen some yield and some rebel.
I have wondered about their lives,

kissed the dead and the awaken.
I have lived by this mystery.
What I tell you now, I tell to the poet
who heals the past with words, who struggles
for understanding. When I say
listen to the needs of the body, I mean
feel the blood's tireless push—
the swollen lungs reckoning into something greater,
or the heart's restless voice—
its song like heat wisps falling.

III

Grandfather

That first year after my father's death, when my brother
was away and my mother started her second job,
my grandfather drove over each night
with his beat-up sax and a bottle of whiskey.
After dinner, he would blow me a long blues,
moonlighter that he was, and I would listen
to the busty sadness of his notes fill the kitchen
the way sweetness filled a room when fruit was ripe.
All night long, he sucked on that reed,
his eyes closed like in the moments before a kiss,
his big shoulders swaying, rolling in a rhythm
of a jazz lullaby. I envisioned the band
behind him, the cheap club veiled in smoke,
the small-time mafia at the tables and the drunks
at the bar. I listened with the minor authority of one
who loved and believed in his grandfather
and not the few dollars clenched in his fist at three a.m.;
the man who crooned the night away like a saint,
who pressed on, who kept imagining.

The Wolf and the Mastiff

How he spent
those years, his breath
pressed firmly
against the lacquered reed, tongue
tucked slightly underneath, a French kiss,
blowing blues, doo-wop,
scat knifing the air with its hot chatter,
while his brother, the postal carrier,
blistered from a nine-to-five stint
on concrete, trapped
in polyester, the leash drawn tightly,
haunches at heel. I imagine
their arguments at the kitchen table, all passion
and gesture—the need to play riffs,
the obligation of family—
and their final parting, my grandfather
leaping from routine
into that lean, blue haze,
prowling the nights with his horn
and bottle, refusing to surrender
to the light
his brother was blinded by.

The Smudge

You walk cracked paths
of scarcity,
stateless wanderer,
having chased after fortune's thread.
Factories spun
not gold, but the wool and sweat
of its brethren,
burning oily heat,
ethnic refineries.
Legends of streets paved
with ivory blackened
with cheap labor,
pressed by
unshaven men and foreign tongues
who provided for the bellies
of their obligation.
Great repatriate,
tears don't buy dime soup.
Yet you walk just the same,
a smudge on society's hand,
peddling the songs and stories
that flutter against deaf ears.

Fearing the Elements

I. Fear of Land

It's this you wait for—
that moment alone
when out on the beach,
the sand is a ribbon of lies,
and it's the tide you wait for—
positive the surf
holds all answers
somewhere deep
within its folding.
Once, you thought this
to be true:
the beach as endless
as the ocean it touches,
meeting at the shoreless point
where dissolution is formed
in the sweep back to sea.
And then you saw the jetty
with its long, powerful arm
split and crack
under the concussive smacks
of waves, rock chunks
slipping helplessly
beneath its tumult.
And then it came to you—
The sea is the one tangible,

faithless, unyielding,
makeshift in its indifference,
overwhelming in attitude,
improvident, invincible.

II. Fear of Water

Drowning in its purest form:
lungs burning, the need
for oxygen stabbing at
the walls of the throat,
the cry that forms and dies
at its origin.
Only the salt's sharp cut
is evident, shooting
into the mouth,
suffocating one hope
after another.
And all the while
it's this you feel—
the solitude
of slipping down further
into a foreign sea,
a fathomless descent
where furor and struggle
meld into one fluent grief,
the blackness of all premises,
and your fears,
anonymous.

III. Fear of Air

A silence so overwhelming
that even the gulls
with their strained cries
fear its presence.
These scavengers, thieves,
let's just say it—
rats of the sky—
glide in its movements,
always a stretch
out of reach.
But when there is no wind,
no breeze, no current,
when the air sits
like something watchful,
these same gulls claw
the sun-burnt shore,
clutching desperately
the sand that sneaks
between their toes.
They sense in the stillness
something vaguely familiar,
like a religion learned
but too distant to remember.
They see in its emptiness
something omnipresent;
a cloudless region
that towers above them—
a thick, blue nothing

that lacquers beach and sea alike,
a place south of heaven
where nothing stirs
or flies.

IV. Fear of Fire

Prometheus saw it first;
the intoxicating blaze dancing
before his eyes, jewel-like,
each flame a jagged tongue
lapping the air above.
His fingers first touched
its angry form, tips blistering,
swelling in ignorance,
his shriek strangled
as a vulture's cry.
For this, he was chained,
armed only
with an unborrowed vision,
his innards devoured
by these same black predators.
The beach at night
is as dark as a vulture's back.
The fire before me
consumes my vision.
It jerks side to side,
its slender fingers clawing
upwards, the act of
the drowning.
For a moment,
my eyes lose themselves
in the bittersweet relationship
between fire and man, the center
blooming hot and white

like a star.
I see in its frenzy
a familiar past as well as present;
a chaotic treading,
lost histories manifested
into one complete biography
of flame.
Like the Titan, my hand
stretches out
to touch its mystery.
When I pull back,
my fingers are burned.

Kissing the Blind

In the park, next to the monuments
whose stark glory diminishes in the sun,
an old woman sits alone on a bench.
Her hands hold a sign—*help me,*

I'm blind—its letters twisted
in uneven shapes, smudged like squashed insects.
Beneath her naked feet rests
a dented metal cup, silver and copper
loose in its belly. I approach her
as I had approached a sedated lion
when I was six, biting my lip,
inching forward slightly, afraid.
I looked through the dark bars
where the lion sat sprawled out, his face
expressionless, vacant. I remember
the depths of his eyes as he watched everything
without blinking, as if his head was stuck to a plaque
on a wall. And yet there was never a question
of strength, the powerful jaws that hung
so slack, the vicious paws, the mane
that caught the wind with its terrible authority.
I ran away crying.
And yet, because what I now know
I learned then,
I must go and give her a kiss
the way my brother made me
eventually pet the lion, my young fingers

stretched out, trembling, touching the thick,
mustard fur, tickling behind the ears.
And so, I lean over the woman's frail frame
and plant my lips over the lid of each
empty eye, looking deeply into this face I fear,
crying the hysterical shrieks that a child cries
when he knows he's been bad;
giving up his tears
until all is forgiven.

The Secret

When my grandmother was asleep, her fingers
swollen from rolling pasta all day,
I waited up and listened for my grandfather,
weaving home from jazz and whiskey.
I lay on the couch, staring out the window, the stars
spilled across the night sky, each constellation
suspended blues notes. Usually, I heard him first,
shuffling up the sidewalk, saxophone cradled in his arm
like an infant son, Holiday's *Lover Man* on his lips,
turning the knob gently, stepping inside. Each night,
I waited for this image of my grandfather: hair swept back
like a seal's fur, oil black; Errol Flynn moustache,
and the Lucky tucked behind his ear
waiting to be sucked down to forefinger and thumb.
I wasn't prepared for the woman on his arm, the whispers,
his touch on her cheek, or the kiss that followed.
I watched him undo the buttons on her blouse
the way he practiced a blues scale, as if each note
counted for something greater than himself;
spreading the silk wings away from her chest, her skin
clean and white as the moon. He looked up at me,
his eyes red with alcohol, and winked—
an age-old ritual passed down from the fires
of civilization, father to son, man to man—
and I blinked back, unsure of what I'd seen,
unable to make sense of the sorrow inside me, this body
in which his secret lives.

Dreams of Dancing

And there is this special likeness
to the woman on the wall
and my grandmother's face.
A certain knowing,
as if to say, *yes dear,*
I was there,
and the more I stare,
the more I know about her—
dreamer, dancer,
would-be Rockette.
And this painting
bears this woman
who sews with thimble
and needle the way
my grandmother does,
looping each thought
with her hand,
her mind lost in the stitching
the way feet are lost
in the steps of a dance.
My grandmother dreams of dancing.
She dreams of being graceful
and slender
and wearing red dance shoes.
She dreams out of herself.
She pretends.
She rocks in her chair
like a pendulum

on a clock
or a metronome.
She sways as rhythm sways—
content, dreamy, full.

What the River Brings Us

(A Walk with my Grandmother)
We walk through the streets together, travelling over
the ancient stones set into the dirty road like markers
of a distant past, the only history that lingers
besides what the river brings us, its current a metaphor
for what we know to be our own lives. If I listen closely,
I can almost hear a desperation within its shadowed movements,
a progression toward somewhere whose resting place
is undetermined, formless as the sun's descent in the horizon,
a destination we can be no surer of than if
we imagined it, pulling from our own dreams. It's been said
that rivers are lonely places, a meandering thread of water
running aimlessly, twisting around, tallying the summation
of our lives until they total balances of nothing. You laugh
as I say this, your withered finger pointing to the deep bend
beside the path, a vain attempt to disprove this theorem
connecting life to a body of water, seeing more perhaps
than a continuance, a shoddy reminder that serves to keep us looking
ahead. All along the river, we pass the hunched forms of old men
strapped to their benches, sentinels over a glassy current,
eyes glazed over like yours, fatigue and age. We follow their gaze,
searching for some secret shining beneath the darkened surface
like a new Lincoln penny, but glimpsing nothing but shadows,
past experience, the fear of what was once but now no longer.
And as we continue to walk through this dying town,
my thoughts slip to those before us who spent their entire lives
travelling this same course, stopping to listen to the silence,
wondering what could be heard, wondering what the river brings us

if we let it, the countless moments spent reasoning why the journey was made, and what was accomplished in leaving, what was worth preserving from the past, and what could ultimately be lost.

Grandfather Drunk

My grandfather believed the best people in the world
lived in bars, propped up on stools, measuring time
by shot glass and beer. He played for them
on weekends, Knick-Knacks on Friday nights,
Bennie's on Saturdays. And the barflies bought drinks
for the small, fat sax player, who listened to the stories
that slurred from their mouths like prophecy.
He'd play them a set and waddle over to the bar
where a bourbon-neat waited, and he would raise
the amber fluid with ritual and respect,
tilting his massive head back, draining the glass.
Into early morning, he sat with these men,
blowing the sad blues of their lives through his horn,
drinking tribute to the dirt and grease
that gleamed off each tired face, spinning
his world so neither the bright nor the bitter came to rest.

The Possibility of Loss

I drive down the street
in hours just before morning,
the light from the lamp posts
twinkling like a tippler's eyes
stumbling home from a night
of drunken reverie.
It's late February,
anniversary of my father's death
and the cold that surfaces now
reminds me when, last summer,
I shivered at the prospect
of another winter,
wanting a change so definite
I believed a move to another city
was in fact better than being
here.
I pass over the corpse of a squirrel
still steaming in the street,
a twisted mass of fur and bone.
Its arm is in angles,
the soft break in its neck
craning for that last breath of air.
I think of that squirrel
and how it must have looked in the headlights,
caught in a sprint across the tar, how it froze there
in an instant of indecision, calculating
the distance back,
how it reacted to a given situation,

preferring the familiarity
of approaching light
to the darkness from which it came, choosing
that which seemed most promising;
its shock when the tire impacted
without warning, the disbelief
as it turned away, betrayed, never having
imagined this possibility of loss.

Watching Drunks Go By

I wonder if they watch
the sun dip its sleepy eye
beneath the skyline, see it sink
slowly as if to say, good night,
lift their faces to its gradual
disappearance, stare in awe
at its bloody remains.
I wonder if they just stagger
around, wrapped in filthy blankets
like some poor disciples
cringing as the air freezes
on their beaten skins,
completely ignoring the red explosion
in the sky,
searching for the corner
that best shields them from the wind,
with enough newspaper
to rest their heads
and pass another night away.

Unspoken Spaces

The trip from the airport
to Montreal is how I envision
Odysseus' trip back to Ithaca
after a hero's journey,
heart swelling in anticipation
of homecoming. This city is unlike any
I have seen, a mélange of old Europe
and the new world, accented
with its own *je ne sai qua.*
Each time I come to Montreal
to escape what I'm missing back home—
the possibilities of what could be
and what could happen
twisted in the interchange of English
and French-Canadian.
Last year, I met a girl.
Spirited and decisive, she showed me
the Montreal that escapes tourists' eyes—
the undercurrent of those "in the know"—
areas where shadows are not places to hide,
but places to be—the night ending
in a fountain of champagne
whose cork was sheared off
by the edge of a saber.
How can you explain a moment like that
with words?
Sitting in a coffee shop overlooking
Le Maissoneuve, the college girls

walk by, chattering in an excitement
reserved for those whose dreams
are still tangible. Their voices ebb
and flow like some vocal tide
rising in a susurrus before a final sweep
back to sea.
And then it's quiet again.
Tonight, I will walk the streets
of St. Catherine and Peel, past
the high-end bars and the strip shows,
one body amidst a throng
whose purpose seems limitless,
wonder etched into each face
as if by wanting something so bad
is the only way to achieve it.
Five days ago,
I walked with my grandfather the same way
until silence settled firmly in the moments
that seemed unbridgeable,
because the unspoken spaces between us
are the moments when we say the most,
whether it's in a furtive glance or pregnant pause,
those poignant instances that say more
than words will ever allow.

My Grandfather in a Shot of Whiskey

He liked it this way because it was quick—
because, with one tilt,
it was gone, vanished, *abracadabra*.
And what he liked most was what a splash
could do, clawing its way back up
his throat after impact, spreading fire.
Fifteen years after his death,
I drink his drink—two fingers
of rail whiskey, whore's scotch,
neat, no ice. It goes down
like bees stinging,
and I remember his face
after he used to swallow, squinting
from the bite and kick. He drank best
alone, left to his bottle and his thirst,
fragments of Coltrane in the background,
tongue tipped bitter with smoke.
He loved to make it last, weaving dizzy
in the night until only the glass remained,
and he'd lift it to his face and view
the world through its thick eye,
blurring the details around him,
shadow and music spinning in the air,
out of nothing, into nothing,
scat on his lips like a swear.

Saxophone Lesson

In the bedroom where he spent hours blowing
bop and swing, I grimace with the blues of a body
broken in clubs where smoke misted up
from tables and knives settled old scores;
where the unemployed sat like so much shattered glass
swept up and unused, discarded by the higher-ups.
My tongue still tastes his whiskey on the reed, the chewed
grooves, the sigh and growl from my gut bleating.
I'd never die for my art, B-flat, wondering
which dents struck the loan shark's head
and which were the result of his own drunken mishaps.
It's almost a parable within itself, this heartbreak
and debt, this longing for the wrong thing.
For a chance to play his sax, at the end of the night,
he'd scrape his tips into his pocket and listen
to the sound they made on the way home.

Playing Cards

(My Grandmother's Story)
In the kitchen, the light from the windows
angling through the blinds, dust glittering
in its beams, we sit at the table,
deck of cards between us. One by one, you flash
each face, the Italian symbols as exotic
as the fistful of *lire* you produced one day,
colorful as a parrot's feathers, thick as cardboard,
impossible to shuffle. You want to teach me *scioppa*,
the game the peasants play when they return
from the fields, mud still drying in the furrows
of their palms, skin leathered from too much sun—
betting under candlelight, wax melting into itself
in white puddles, the card suits screened in shadow.
You tell a story about your brother Pepe,
a man whose appetite for cards was large enough
to swallow eggplant, and the hours he spent
hustling lire from the farmers, sweeping
the tarnished change and rumpled bills
into the ladle of his hand; how he played the odds,
calculating each throw, collecting diamonds, winning trick
after trick, his take piled before him like semolina sacks.
You tell how he faced a fire when they cornered him
in the barn, the jaundiced mark of losing imbedded
beneath their eyes, pockets run dry and barren;
how these same men scarred him a cheat,
heating a coin until it glowed white-hot with rage,
forcing it against his cheek. And still, each night back

89

from pushing oxen, the tattoo of distrust
beaming off his face, he played; fanning the cards,
the *sete bella*, lucky seven, emblazoning his eyes—
its seven stars budding in the presage of mid-bloom—
that promise to be something more.

Breakfast at Metro 29

I spend a lot of time here now that you're away.
The waitress recognizes my face,
her eyes bright with acknowledgement.
She leads me to our table where
I drink coffee after coffee,
substituting nourishment with caffeine.
My appetite has vanished since you left,
leaving me crumpled and stained,
an unpaid check.
When you return, we'll eat like we used to:
scrambled eggs and flapjacks smothered
in maple syrup, the butter sweetening
on our tongues. You'll order
freshly squeezed O.J. and greasy home fries,
and we'll feast while we reassemble
our lives like we used to—
one forkful at a time.

Strangers

We are strangers by any standard—
similar waves but unfolding
in separate tumults, sinking into the sand's uniformity.
Or else, like clouds we drift—
not melting, not fusing, but locked in thought,
in looks that aspire for those dreams
hidden by fear, that single most feeling.
We tread, slowly first, rising up and up, curling those dreams
that lie between us, the clouds, and the sea,
molding each one into tiny wishes
eloquent as an angel's sigh; we ascend, further and further
into light, into the very heavens
where cherubim sing like divine troubadours,
their song echoing the song of tides
that climaxes in a symphony of foam and thunder,
each wave undulating in unrestricted harmony,
their collisions embracing the shore
before dissipating in sweeping arcs
white as comets. It's here that the water and cumulus alike
are drawn together and rooted,
rooted by the wanting that causes our dreams
to dream, our thoughts to breathe as one,
this same wanting that lies deep
within the place within us that cries out
wanting to know your face and mine.

Communion

In summer, in humidity
and too much sweat, and hot, hot things
rising from the streets, I watch
the bums in the park, nipping
off a bottle shrouded in paper.
They pass a cigar back and forth,
a Round Table of tobacco and liquor,
no thought but the next drink
and the amount short
on a forty-ounce beer,
always the thirst
because it's liquid the body loses,
so liquid the body must take.
They fumble their pockets for pennies,
seven in one, eleven in another,
pool it together in a pile
of copper. What remains
is the drawing of lots,
who's to go, and who's to stay,
spinning in the afternoon
like a dizzy memory.
And when he returns,
the rest marvel at the tin in his hands,
not a gold cup but something a carpenter
might drink from, sipping and passing,
sipping and passing—
this is His body,
it was given up for you.

Skid Row Serenade

(My Grandfather's Song)
I. The Homeless Drinks
He doesn't want to forget. That time is over,
the self-mourning, self-scrutiny,
blurred reflection somewhere in the back-wash.
The drunk on Park and Elm knows his past
and knows he can't escape it,
although he's tried, bourbon after bourbon
neat, no ice, Friday nights that slipped
into Monday mornings. Now he just sits
as he's supposed to sit, eyes sunk back
into the shadow of his face, a fine film
glazed over his body like a new skin.
He sips his whiskey as if each swallow
brings with it a new memory; as if finishing
the entire bottle breaks you down
then builds you a new life.
II. The Homeless Eats
The food isn't there. The fingernails
clotted with grease and dirt
burrow beneath the trash folds
like maggots through a decayed body.
First some orange rinds, some newspaper,
the acrid stench of catfish;
then some scraps from last night's dinner—
fat, grizzle, maybe an empty tuna can.
The backwash in a bottle if he's lucky,
a mouth-full of eighty proof, anything

to hide the taste; maybe something sweet,
something strong. Something worth swallowing
that won't be thrown up in an hour.
You've seen this man,
stormed past his bags in the street,
kicked his teeth in. You've
slapped away his cup
with your eyes, pushed him
to the back of your mind,
a vague memory;
laughed at his filth,
cringed under the stench
of his urine, turned your ears
from his ragged voice.
Murderous son of Adam,
you rise against your kin
with indifference;
you murder your brother every day.
III. The Homeless Sleeps
in something other than dreams, his face
sunk beneath the webbing of his hands,
newspaper stuffed inside his shirt,
a disturbed breath stumbling from his lips.
If I think hard enough, I can remember the stories
of my grandfather who drank so much wine
that he slept in the street for a week, snoring,
his bulbous red nose thick with mucous.
People poked him with a stick or cane
and jumped back as if they had awakened

a bear or sleeping giant.
And now I see him again, my grandfather lost
in tattered sleep, darkness gathered around him
in deep folds, his slumped posture laying
there as if to say, *what is it you see?*
Why do you fear me?

Grandfather's Blues

When your liver gave, we took you
to the hospital, your taste for scotch
becoming too large to process.
Those last few months, your thirst
outgrew the drink or two in between sets.
You pulled from the bottle,
letting the whiskey pour over
your teeth like a wash of sugar.
There was no more strut left in your sax,
no more bluster and pop, blues-
induced visions. No more Coltrane riffs
in rooms where jazz replaced sound
with improvisation and myth.
You swapped Baker for Beam,
trading one discipline for another,
playing out your version of the body dark,
the IV dripping into your vein, a mood indigo,
one precious note at a time.

Viewing My Grandfather's Body

I kneel before you
and peer into the box
where you lay fast asleep,
the stone slab of your body
cool and white as marble.
I follow your line—shoulder
elbow, arm, wrist—
to where your saxophone presses
into your side the way a pistol
presses into a soldier's hip;
and I can tell by the way your eyes hide
behind their lids that you are lost beneath
the dreamy blues of a jazz tune.
I touch your face—
the skin pulled tight and wrinkle-free,
the large skull covered
by that impossibly smooth veil,
and think of each small death
you suffered those nights
blowing brass to a handful
of customers until 3 am,
taking your pay in whores and booze.
Looking at you stilled and pressed
as a sheet of music,
I see no frustration or fear;
only the mythic face of the artist triumphant
dreaming a steady tempo, an upbeat rhythm,
jamming in a session that will never end.

Smoke in the Afterlife

funny how things come about
when you don't see them
or can't
but they come
just the same
seeing you that last time
on the steps
cigarette in hand
smoke leaving your lips
in a cool blue jet—
I had one too
inhaling deeply
each puff
a knot of something
I couldn't tell you
my chest tightened
and burned
exhaling slowly
each ring
some part of you
I couldn't let go.

Acknowledgments

The author would like to thank the following journals for publishing these pieces:

"The Beating" — *Soundings East*

"The Apology" — *Mediphors*

"That Sunday" — *The GW Review*

"Dreams of Dancing" — *Mobius*

"Playing Cards" — *Ship of Fools*

"My Brother Speaks" — *11th Muse Press*

"Angels on the Head of a Pin" — *11th Muse Press*

"Grandfather" — *Whiskey Island Press*

"Grandfather's Blues" — *The Plastic Tower*

"Grandfather Drunk" — *Voices West*

"My Grandfather in a Shot of Whiskey" — *Natural Bridge*

"The Saxophone Lesson" — *Brilliant Corners*

"The Secret" — *Barkeater*

"My Father Asleep" — *Mediphors*

"Better" — *Visions*

"Anniversary of My Father's Death" — *Raven Chronicles*

"Fisherman's Daughter" — *Iron Horse Literary Review*

"Becoming my Mother" — *Black and White*

"Poem for an Unknown Father" — *Wavelength*

"Witch" — *Common Ground Review*

"Mischief Night" — *California Quarterly*

"Childhood Rushes Toward Death" — *The Moon Magazine*

"Retelling the Story" — *The Moon Magazine*

"Becoming My Mother" — *Open: Journal of Arts and Letters*

"Kissing the Blind" — *Gival Press*
"The Homeless Eats" — *Gival Press*
"The Product" — *The Pangolin Review*

Made in the USA
Middletown, DE
10 February 2020